A FINE LINE

A collection of poetry

© Dianne Bates

For my dearest Billy

Contents

People

House Caller

Stars burst in the sky
above the valley
where he is quietly walking,
stalking.
There is no way he can be
shut out; he is a
shock to the blood.
He wants to know her,
finds clues here
in photos on walls
where she smiles at him,
the child's drawings of her
stick-thin
and so attractive.
Even the laundry reveals her -
uniforms, ironed,
crisp as his daring,
under-things splayed like thighs -
petticoats, panties, and bra -
delicate as the hold he has on her.
He sees everything. But
he cannot see into
the mind of the woman
who placed
the china dolls in a cabinet
pirouetting
almost touching
the jars of potpourri
on the window sill

tamarillos ripening,
patterned with slits
the blind makes.
In half-light, late at night
he wills her to become
as real to him
as onions sprouting in a tub
their layers peeling,
as solid as spuds.

Luna, Aged One

I watch her grow, register
every new movement
today calling my name
for the first time
allowing me to hold her, but then
she reads something
just beyond my shoulder
and shrieks
I wonder what compels
that trapeze-flip of her scream
her gasping face
the twisting of her body
I hand her back
to the safety of Mummy's arms
where she settles
she loves that calm devotion
the gentleness of touch
the security of breasts,
the throwing up and tickling
the face-pulling of her besotted dad
their life without her would be
as empty as space
they see her gestures
I'm hungry, I want, come here, go away
she cannot mutter the word for Love
but it is there in her face
her small but powerful hands
stroking Daddy's bearded cheeks
her mouth poised for a kiss

she has unguessed wisdom
that unites her parents, attracts
the smiles of everyone
with her wild and precious life
one day, when we least expect it,
she will fly.

Kathleen Julia

Molten earth, spinning through space
I expel you.
You take your place in the elements
moon, a ghost eclipsed by this planet.
We neither give our own light,
it is always so between mother and offspring,
so what need,
                my child,
                    of your sacrifice?
For you, no panoply of air
to shield your death
by that incandescent star
        falling,
           falling
                through hallways of your
                    life's unopened doors.
The tides have not ceased
nor the seasons.
I can do nothing but gaze at you now,
white sterile melon.

Widower

They brought her encased in wood
to this lonely plot and laid it deep
smothered it with clods
wept and prayed.
The mound felt the moon
the white moths of stars
fluttered about
the widower grieved,
picked flowers -
small yellow suns -
and set them on marble.
He is here each Sunday,
preferring her company
to the cold kitchen
routine of papers
and she, warm corpse, awaits him.
He polishes her stone
pulls weeds rooted in loss
and feels her reaching
to touch some part of him
slowly cooling.

Seasons change and earth,
and a man's grief,
plucking him from life
as flowers on a grave,
will fade and wilt in time.
Passions dead are soon revived
his empty bed filled.

Under the sky
weeds grow green and long,
the headstone weathers.

The Singing Teacher

We, whose words live alone like hermits,
try to adjust our positions
to the arc and tenor of a frozen world.
We wander in and out
of each other's mouths
in search of a tune;
find there is always a difference
between the wish
and the granting,
a sad gap like a pause in song.
We lose words as we try to remember how to speak.

The time has come to confess
that which we cannot solve ourselves,
that which must be shared.
Behold her –
a soul who bestows music and love!
Sad choir in search of voice,
we flutter to her,
and listen as she teaches us to travel with feelings,
to open our mouths and pierce
the frozen quiet with trust.
She asks more from us than we never knew to ask.
Sometimes in winter, love causes
tuneless voices to sing
like spring-time birds.

Hang Glider

Some days
He wants to glide,
to perform a dance of sorts
at the edge of the abyss
before launching his body
into space
Lately he's been dreaming it often,
imagining giant lungs
beneath him,
drawing in breath,
and exhaling into the blue.
He's there now
riding on exhilaration like a drug,
giddy with freedom.
Never wanting to let go
of this moment
he feels lifted beyond
anything he ever dreamed
the tie of marriage
his role as father
the embracing arms
of his future.
This is it, oh boy!
he hollers to the echoing world
and an open-armed air-god
rushes up to greet him,
takes him to a place
beyond his imagining.
He would like the journey to last forever,

but he's a realist,
he's had his vision of Heaven:
now he knows Destiny;
they are on the friendliest of terms.
He's coming down now
the clock ticking
a knuckle raps on his door
he meets his appointment
landing on terra firma with
a grin wide as the horizon.
He's here now
locked to the swivel chair
in the venetian-blinded office
inhaling and exhaling
concentration
minutes dripping from the clock,
listening to the wounds
of the life-wearied.

The Bushman

for Max Williams

Disappearing into silence
as he often does,
he strides the hills
loves the freedom
of space
he never knew in prison.

The morning clean as
bone stripped bare,
he haunts the forest of
Dr George Mountain Tanja via Bega,
the air ripped with birdcall
watches an eagle
raising its wings then falling,
swooping out of sight,
hears bell birds
clinking non-stop, and
bickering starlings.
A flock of birds leaves
the side of the mountain
black against the azure sky
wheeling to some far destination.
Like mist departing
in the enormous dawn
among autumn brush
he is alone in his kingdom
surrounded by life.

She is convinced she is dying

alone in the hospital bed
between visitors
isolation and terror radiating
as the oxygen tube
works its miracle
filling her clenched lungs.
Earlier, the doctor delivered doom,
sympathetic but doing his job,
'Nothing more can be done
your heart is swollen,
beating below par
not long left.'
Now there is no-one
to share this news

When will a visitor come
to repeat the verdict
watch faces shocked
Hear words, 'Of course not,'
'You're not at the end!'
'Better than you've been in years.'
The doctor is re-called,
the relatives fire questions
'Surely not!'
Medical notes again consulted.
'Oh,' he says, 'There's been a mistake,
wrong chart
she's to be discharged
taken home tomorrow.'

Such a small mistake. And months later
the only thing left of that day
of the hours alone in that room.

In the Beginning

The sun has dropped from the sky.
You peer into the girl's uplifted eyes,
Her mind engraved with belief:
'Love cannot reside here,
It is a stranger.'
Her tongue is steel, and, you suspect,
the heart.
Undaunted,
You reach out, think
If only this were enough,
the offering of hands
to help unload grief,
heal the soul that has not yet
learned
love.
Endless mother, physician,
you begin to undo the tongue
like bandages,
release memories
too powerful to escape from.
Sparks begin to rise
like stars being born.

After

(for PM)

Days unloop and you are trapped
in your car
homeless and unwanted.
Beyond, a myriad of stars flickers
like campfires from your youth
you huddle into the blanket stolen from your father's bed
your last faithful friend
your dog
nuzzled against you.
Night draws you further
towards another empty day.
Restless hours later
surfers pass by, calling,
you prick up your ears
like a tired hound,
watch the sun rise over Sandon Point.
You want the world to be sweet beyond measure
but love you took for granted
has burned
the push and pull of hours
the grind of togetherness
you demanded too much
gave so little
damned yourself to the sly outlines of abandonment
the sun like a massive wall.

When I am Old

I will change my face,
shave my eyebrows,
crop my hair so all can see
the scars,
dye what is left
a bright blue
zigzagged with red.
People in the street will stare,
I will frighten small children
with my razor-teeth smile,
nibble on babies' toes
and kick cats,
poison snarling dogs
I will swear at bureaucrats
I bowed to in a past life
their bones juicy as spit.
Those who loved me once
will turn aside
but I will be ready for that
and turn first.
I will have need of no-one.
Love will not figure
in my life's equation,
only freedom -
masses of it -
to hell with rules and conventions!
When I am old
I will never lie down.

Relationships

First Kiss

Pandemonium
this was our house when the old man exploded
hurling vicious words with plates, knives, pots
whatever came to his brick-hard hands.
We scrambled but
I was trapped
my face under this boot
blood poured over my skin
and tears and snot
and then
he was gone.
Quiet and peace descended
we picked ourselves up
our eyes not connecting
rearranging the wreckage
when someone knocked
we stood like death
my mother gestured,
I answered
he was a boy from my school
straight-backed
usually cool but
this day shock in his eyes
as it was in mine
standing there, witness to disarray,
to my distress
Mum let me walk with him a while
in the bush where birds sang
and warm light blanketed us.

He did not ask and I did not tell,
my tongue glued in my mouth.
Instead, for the first time, he wrapped
his arms around my shivering body
and found my lips with moist, gentle kisses.
In my hunger
he brought me hope, and,
for those short euphoric moments,
I was set free from my unlovely life.

When we met

I rushed headlong
into flames,
so long in loneliness
I didn't see the signs —
Caution
Beware
Go back.
Soon,
trapped,
I found myself
in a world
random as desire
clenched in a fist
of belonging.
Pregnant
I was buried chin-deep
in days that were
a gun hammer
cocked-back
in readiness
for his trigger-fast temper.
Life wrestled everything
into itself
the dark was intolerable.
When at last,
shattered,
I could take no more
and fled
it was like dawn-breaking,
the narrow sky shifting
into endless horizon.

Just Married

Day bore witness to a farce.
A blue frock disguised my pregnancy.
You, black-suited.
Ironic really,
that suit bought on credit,
waiting for our friends to arrive,
impatient to get it over with.
The knoll of social pressures ringing
in our ears,
'We close at four. Do hurry please.'
That momentous decision
asking two strangers in the street
to witness.
Then emerging into the city,
eating our breakfast at the local pub
(Wondering if we could pay the bill,
and whether the car would get us home.)
Our honeymoon weekend,
the landlord knocking for the rent.
We pretended not to be there.

My Child

Tugging your ear,
a toy bear under your other arm
you stare at me
every day in my office
wearing my old shoes.
Like life, they never fitted.
Forty and more years later
I have forgotten the scent
of your two-year-old skin,
your lips skimming my face.

Today

I shall consider
A major shard of experience
which has shaped
my adult life:
the hospital ward,
her skull so foreign
swollen
wrapped in bandages.
I am now
a newly orphaned mother
my child ready for the oven.
My descent into grief
is marked by the decades.
Her dead face haunts me.
I have more photos of her
as a corpse
from the autopsy
than I have of her alive.
Always, always she will be smaller
than the words 'I miss you.'

On Claremont Street

My neighbours are noisy
above the ceiling
of my unit
filled with toucans.
They tap, bang, bash for hours.
I listen to James Galway playing flute
(Bach is best)
then cycle to the pool
swim twenty laps.
Back home
stare into the computer screen,
write a sentence,
then some more,
give birth to dragons.
The banging, bashing, banging
bashing
goes on and on and on.
I drive a hatchet
into their feeble brains.
Later I plead guilty to justifiable homicide.

Making Changes

Some days, as years creep
and seep into my aging bones,
I no longer feel alive in my skin
as I did when I was young,
loose-limbed, wild and free.
Now my skin is wrinkling
I'm morphing into someone
I don't recognise
accepting the soothing monotony
of daily life
the structured string of days.
I tell myself to slough off this decline
stop accepting the tedium of ordinary days
stop being alarmed by the enormity of the end
I need to wean myself from the teat
be afraid no longer,
no longer retreat
I need to recapture moments of freshness
reinvigorate, fill my head with the blue of sky
not the little bits flashing by
come alive with the joy of newness
bring back youthful energy
and hope.

Enemy

This is she
who should be
Enemy.

Zooming in I see close-up
her fine cheek down.

So,
this is she
whom he pursues,
declares he has always wanted.

I'd love to give her forty kilos
(just to make her a worthy opponent, you understand)
and halitosis,
disposition of a bitch
in season.

But there she is
smiling all the way to Florida,
10 in a bikini
bakes Sunday roasts
cute as apple pie.

Sweet sister, I would like
to suck your marrow
crush your bones
erase you from his randy brain.

Instead,
I shall give you
these love letters,
the ones he sent to me
only last week.

What I Told Her

'What should I say?' asks the old lady,
'to my grand-daughter,
'who's unbearably sad, unreachable?'
'She is there,' I advise,
as one who knows.
'Tell her,
"Yes, for now your world is bleak
and hope too difficult to imagine,
impossible to mend.
There seems only this moment,
too awful to describe."'
'Take her hand, friend,
'stroke her hair,
'be the adult she needs.
'Tell her, "Your feelings are not facts.
'For the moment your mind is ill.
'To heal, you need your physician, medications
'And though right now
'all seems impossible
'time will heal."'
'Tell her, "One day you will
'see light,
'hear music,
'laughter
'even welcome the future:
'then you will know
'you have been brave
'to have recovered from this awful trial
'and too,

you will know you are loved.'"
My friend,
Though she might now seem to be deaf,
your grand-daughter needs
to hear your words;
Your promises, as she knows
from your past,
are true.
Keep telling her
of your love,
of her potential,
of hope.
One day she will
Thank you.

Imagining the Future

Lost completely in daydreams
day after day and walled
within these four rooms
long winters drawling past
and summers hot and endless as hell
it becomes easy over time and daily habit
to imagine another lover
a man moving to a different
more romantic tempo.
In my mind,
it's as though a hand erases
the long dreary days
everything changes
I carve out new shapes
that excite
and invent a stranger
valued for his novelty
create an innocent first world
with marvels ahead, not knowing
that unplanned patterns will eventually
make the same patterns
(this becomes evident when I am much older,
when skies grow a little more forgiving
and clouds lay in one flat, unrelieved bank).

Somehow Surviving

Roaring in my dreams
I wake every day slashed
with unspeakable
sadness
thinking
of you who thinks
only of me
with contempt;
I see it
in your cruel eyes
considering me like
a defective thing
worthless as addiction.
My body feels shrunken
and carved, my heart
a relentless muscle
opening and closing
stubborn as time.
As the day churns by
I stumble along the thin wire of need
unnavigable sorrow
when oh when will it ever end?

Love

That first flush

of love surging
like an orgasm
through my body, stroking
every nerve every cell
impossible really to describe
how it overpowers,
like mainlining heroin
the hit, the smack
releasing me
into other dimensions
I never knew
pleasurable
of course
not the first hit but again
and again I'm so addicted
can't break free
hold me tightly don't
ever leave

Breathing together

You say you can't sleep
until you hear my snores.
You rub my back
as a parent with a small child
till sleep comes.
Sometimes I wake
and you are gone.
When I wander into your office
you say, 'I've only been up
for minutes.'
We are so in tune with each other
we make the most harmonious song
When was the moment you
stepped into my heart
and claimed it entirely?

Marriage

like landscape
has a distinct geography
depths and heights
so much to negotiate
the smooth hills of routine
the creek beds,
like our days
that flow
to the ocean
with its constant and reliable tides
and then there are forests
exotic and deep
loosing yourself in them
the lakes, deep and clear
you can see all the way
to the very bottom.
Others in marriages have tussling times
but you and I are co-joined
like mountain and valley
that merge
sharing deep comforts,
in harmony with one another
nuzzling, nestling
connected.
That we have survived so many years
- and joyous ones at that -
is a miracle
like the earth
sometimes taken for granted.

Nesting Doves

Among the vines
of the passionfruit
a pair of doves weaves
a nest,
a future.
Colour of underfelt
the male
with too-heavy twig
battles air-currents.
Like you, dear one,
those hell-long years
when my brain was on fire,
when doctors despaired
and departed,
hospitals too,
the world...
The dove lets the twig fall.
The vine sighs
like years passing.
Days later I notice
the nest
abandoned
the doves re-building elsewhere.
The sky is as blue as hope.

Analysing love

Let me undress love
carefully remove its onion-skin layers…
love grows in such haphazard ways
the tones of our voices,
squeezes in the dark
hugs in the kitchen
your knuckles rubbing my aching back,
partners for the long haul.
'I am the weight'
You said one morning
in bed, 'You are the balloon
'always trying to lift me;'
'I anchor you,
'prevent you from escaping
'to a future of doom.'
'You were sleepy
when you mumbled this,
eyes closed
and I, wide awake,
mind fluttering in all directions
anticipating the day.
Soon my chatter wakened you
and we talked
for a long time
mostly about books we were reading
and our plans for the day.
We never run out of things
to talk about.

My husband

For Billy

Your hands remind me of prayer
your fingers
shift mountains
gentle me into sleep;
your face so familiar
I know it even
when we are apart.
There's a photo I took
when you were far away
wandering,
behind you an abstract painting
of floating clouds
colours swirling
a fantasy landscape.
Every intimate contour
of you
is a tiny spyhole
into a vast universe.

Since his fall

smashing his teeth, gashing his chin
he does not trust
has become frail
moves
awkward and angular
sloth-like
and yet he has resolved
that old age will not slow him
so he moves his body hour after hour
hobbling along the flat path
beside our home
(one hundred laps is an hour)
lifts weights
finds comfort in repetition
trying to strengthen the chalk of his bones
the flaccidity of muscle
he honours his noble soul
by not giving up,
hangs on like death
I stand on the sidelines and cheer.
Oh darling
I admire your fire
trust yourself –
you will prevail.

Slipper Love

Life goes on and
you fill the spaces
the best you can.
With time
the love you once had
with edges
and complications
changes,
becomes smoother and simpler.
One day
you realise
those spaces are
happy ones
your love
and you
have aged and
now you fit together
comfortably
like old slippers
warming each other.

For the Moment

For HM

One day it will vanish,
how I felt when I was overwhelmed by you,
but for now I want to touch the edges of your face,
soft and gentle as Mother Love.
Contained within you is an entire continent of understanding
a heart that makes the sun rise and set.
This is the tender moment of all –
your arms enclosing my brittle parcel
of bones and organs and fear.
The comfort is exquisite.
I escape the crush of the world
leave my body where it is, and float.
The moon sucks in and then expels the planet's tides.

Unwinding a coil in my heart
you become the one green blade in a never-ending desert.

Loss and Madness

Grief and grief and grief

Since I last saw you
grief has speared into me,
anchoring me,
it seems it will not shake
free
the loss of you has become
unbearable and timeless
like a sulky-eyed shadow
which stalks every day

In this world where jets fly into buildings
the future without you is unchartered

Downcast and grave

I wandered the school grounds
in my final years
wholly lost
hopeful of friendship
but finding none
anxiety etched my face
my mind filled
with god-awful secrets
helpless to disclose.
Nobody noticed
or if they did, enquired
why my mouth,
opened to speak,
was soundless.

The Rifle

leans against the fridge
it's always there
unless he's shooting
at me
as he did today
when I defended my friend
whom he called a lesbian
and she's not
though what does it matter.

I should take it
tonight
and by the moonlight
in his room
level it at his sleeping head
pull the trigger.

That place

inside of me
needs filling
again and again
can never be sated.
What is it that will come
and sit lightly
and satisfy
and when
I ask again and again
wanting answers
wanting the truth.
But truth is a tired
foot that treads
where it ought not,
is never sure of itself.

Loss

Inside me you crouch
like a bruised shape
forever haunting.
You whisper my name
at night
through endless time.
Daily I feel your rhythms
smell your skin
imagine the imprint of your body.
Every moment
I attempt to tiptoe
away from you,
yet there you are,
galloping across my mind
with footsteps
heavy as my aching need of you.

Take Today

(for NS)

How many times do you have to die
before you are undeniably dead?
Take today for instance:
my mouth suddenly lost words
they tripped and tumbled and tore apart –
there was no bottom to my sadness.
Memories – every past, tormented thought
stalked the boundaries of my mind.
At first, they nibbled
then they gobbled into it.
Juice ran down my mind's grotesque mouth.
It belched like a storm god
unyielding, intent on destruction.

Some days – like today –
the mind performs endless tricks,
runs in many different directions
never staying long enough
to see anything.
It attempts to out-do itself
thumping with terror and despair
ripping with pain sharp as hooks.
Life gets its blade out
hacking at reality.
The mouth is a void
and hope is a word not yet invented.

Alone

Through all my childhood
He thundered,
Smashing my innocence
Branding my mind
with menace.
And too he created a mother
Who shrank into the skirting boards
Until she vanished, and
I was unprotected
Always tottering
On the edge
Of an abyss
Wanting to fall yet
Searching for a grip-hold
And finding none.
Determined to save the only life
I could
For years I lived
In the narrowest crack,
My life a continuous booby-trap.

Chamber of Horrors

Ward downstairs, an inmate howls
interminably.
Woman in 10 moans, chocking phlegm,
snores as a man, clicking loose dentures,
someone protests to nurse,
one minute of shift to go.
Night rotates on this roster.
Remembering Kathleen. Now three years,
pacing hospital halls, timing seconds,
knowing her doom, wired to a respirator
(Tiny wax-like figure),
tiptoeing the waiting room and
screaming inwardly at her death.

Somehow Surviving

Roaring in my dreams
I wake every day slashed
with unspeakable
sadness
thinking
of you who thinks
only of me
with contempt;
I see it
in your cruel eyes
considering me like
a defective thing
worthless as addiction.
My body feels shrunken
and carved, my heart
a relentless muscle
opening and closing
stubborn as time.
As the days churn by
I stumble along the thin wire of need
unnavigable sorrow
when oh when will it ever end?

Confessional

Weeks passed in the therapist's room,
where, weak woman, I turned
Amazonian, loose-limbed
and elephant-strong,
wore an invisible helmet
cast from iron,
and carried arsenal for revenge.
Disguised as a gentle-woman
I oversaw an army
brave as Boudica —
more powerful by far.
For the first time, trusting,
I advanced,
and on a day the stars
aligned, took a rock
and shattered my abuser's skull
pounded his brain,
slimy beyond recognition,
unsheathed my sword --
severed his sick
grinning head,
its serrated tongue,
his torso,
his penis, once dangerous as
a slashing blade.
The truth disrobed,
I stood,
sans shield and weapons,
before my God, the Therapist.

She did not speak
gave no sign
had she heard?
did her heart beat?
was she real?
When the clock closed her door
I left, raw-eyed,
my marrow curdled,
my heart in shards.

Now I wait,
wait for open arms to bind my fragmented soul,
wait for roses to open to the moon,
for midnight skies to be rainbow tinged,
wait for God in this god-forsaken world.

If

If I held a stiletto poised to puncture
my repentant heart
would you, could you
forgive me?
If with this stiletto I were to carve
APOLOGY
so deep it scarred,
would you, could you
forgive me?
In that smiling moment,
hands touching,
my confession whipped your mouth
to a snarl,
you withdrew,
tattooing my mind
with rejection.
All through those scrambling moments
I hoped for
forgiveness:
the words never came.
Later I offered bouquets to your
turned back,
and lay beneath the blanched moon
for the sun that seemed
to live forever
beneath the horizon.
Now I stand naked,
holding a blade to my chest,
waiting

for your deadweight heart
to resuscitate,
for your ice-mouth to thaw,
to command execution,
or,
(dare I hope?)
to pardon.

After-life

All our lives we've tiptoed around it,
from the moment we knew
there was an end
we feared Death but now
let us imagine
it is here with arms wide-spread
and we plunge in;
loved ones behind us mourn our passing
but we are away without a backward glance.
Now imagine that our past shadows have gone
the light here is golden and our now is forever
we've come to the end of what we could ever achieve
and halleluiah, we're here in heaven.
We see the faces of saints whispering prayers
forgiving mistakes we made in life.
Now we are currents flowing
richer by a kind of blessing
clean, whole, calm.
We're dreaming of nothing but goodness
we have no fear, no illness, aging, stress
now that Death has claimed us.
Our world at last is an endless meadow,
where, in a kind of sweet delirium,
we are swirling and singing
nothing stops or jars
in our wonder-filled, carefree world.

Places

Campbelltown

On the highway to Appin
skies bled on Summer nights.
The road hummed to town from cattle grazing,
trucks speeding coal to the coast,
and south of main street,
silent on a bridge,
the ghost of Fisher.
Weekdays we rose at five
blowing balls of warmth into Winter air,
and milking the cows
I sang at the bails,
'Rose Marie, I love you'.
Summer was blowies in the cream
butter that melted,
eggs from gasping hens.
Mrs Tietzel brought the mail
Campbell the bread
the days moved sideways.
Saturday was cricket
or Menangle trots,
swimming at the Woolwash
and the Queen Street shops.
Tub was cockatoo for SP bookies in pubs
and kids lined up at the picture house
game girls rubbing cheeks with bristling boys.
Paspalum brushed the sky
and we forgot ourselves.
In the showground cemetery
beneath the shadow of Ruse

who sowed the first grain
we made rubbings on tombs;
JOHN MACARTHUR, ELIZABETH, R.I.P.
In Mawson Park
the band played *Matilda,*
someone scribbled his mind on toilet walls,
and, beyond trains that steamed to Sydney,
I dreamed a freedom of cities and age.

Hay to Balranald

Nothing grows on this vast, inhuman plain
where brown brittle shrubs
squat on a flat land
still, it is a season for respite
clouds, black as the pupil of messiah's eye
infiltrate sky's blue iris
dragging shadows.
Nothing else moves but my lone car
in an intense burst for home.
Drive on,
drive on,
drive on,
past truck tyres blown at roadside,
black phallic shapes -
goanna, swan, now snake,
and the ground thrusts up
a glass plantation -
long-necked bottles sucked dry.
Nothing survives but driftwood telegraph
posts in this inland sea
struggling erect to belt against the wind.
Tormented fences hold nothing
for miles, miles, miles,
until the straight road becomes master,
sliding its black tongue
into my journey,
whispering,
"Come with me, come with me."

Bega 6.30 am

The early morning coach departs,
a lone seagull skirts the civic centre.

Here, last night, love died
And I take leave with the dawn.

A new sun struggles to assert itself,
merging with the lazy haze of fires.

Housewives cook breakfasts
on fuel stoves:

daylight affirms family and place.

As I head north past the caravan parks
cattle methodically feed knee-deep
in sodden kikuyu,
alert for sound of men
and milking machines.

Cobwebs spun on wire fences
stretch the highway
and fog fuses
with golden ambers –
autumn leaves changing faces
before winter's winnowing mood.

Tomorrow in the city, I decide,
I'll buy a new dress, swap wigs,
step fancy free.

A sign flashes by –
Sydney 395.

Canoeing on Tanja Lagoon

From oyster-crusted rocks launched,
the canoe rides sunken inlets,
furrowing through the lagoon's lip.

We match each other,
slapping the water's
close-mouthed challenge,
each stroke sapping energy.

Across Tanja lagoon the sun goes out.
Night draws us home.
We grin,
sliding into tide
we know
there are times like this that bind.

Dr George Mountain

Bellbirds chink in monotone.
Over granite monoliths
in valleys
waterfalls spill on tree ferns
and delicate maidenhair.

On The Diggings
folk collect wood
for night-time fires.
"Rubbish," the forester said;
chain-sawing for the mill
he left residue.

Near shafts of the thirties
where white men sweated a fever
that was gold
a small family gather left-overs.

Where Birds Fly

All Winter long he knew their call -
vague mating instincts
come to nest again.
The way of the bird, wild dog and boy,
long bamboo fishing poles, things that matter,
he knew them all.
Solitary now, the man stands seaward,
wind traces grey in his hair,
listens to the birds.
A trawler hunts the horizon,
an albatross dangles on a thread of sun
striking a million images across waves.
Seeking a need of his own
he has come back to where
loneliness rides a regular tide
but birds fly free.

www.ingramcontent.com/pod-product-compliance
Lightning Source LLC
Chambersburg PA
CBHW060452160726
47992CB00003B/1194